For my husband, Warwick, and children, Jassie, Nate, and Josh—
all of whom have spent their recent holidays touring convict sites across Australia

ACKNOWLEDGMENTS

I'd like to thank my encouraging publisher and editor, Maryann Ballantyne, for the opportunity to write this book, and the talented team at Walker Books, who helped bring it to life. Professor Lucy Frost, from the Female Convicts Research Group, and Ken Lee, from the Port Arthur Historic Site, provided expert guidance, while Bruce Kirkman and Deb Kirkman gave valuable feedback on early versions of the text.

First U.S. edition 2015

Library of Congress Catalog Card Number 2014952796
ISBN 978-0-7636-7326-0

APS 20 19 18 17 16 15
10 9 8 7 6 5 4 3 2 1

Printed in Humen, Dongguan, China

This book was typeset in Bembo.

Candlewick Press
99 Dover Street
Somerville, Massachusetts 02144

visit us at www.candlewick.com

CONTENTS

GREAT SOUTHERN LAND

Most people, at some point, look beyond their hometown and try to imagine what's out there. When we do this today, we often think about the stars in the night sky and maybe even aliens from unknown planets. But if you were living in Europe hundreds of years ago, the world would have been a mystery. The only way to travel to distant lands was by ship, and these dangerous voyages could take many years.

As sails and ships improved, Europeans were able to voyage to faraway countries to trade for goods they couldn't get at home. Sometimes, when they sailed into the Southern Hemisphere, they were blown onto an unknown coast by wild storms. European sailors did not know anything about this strange region, except that there had always been legends of a Great Southern Land—one that was as large as the vast northern continents, like Europe and North America.

The first recorded European visit to Australia was in 1606 when a Dutch captain, Willem Janszoon, landed on what we now call the Gulf of Carpentaria. Over the next few decades, around fifty more European ships bumped into this continent, and by the mid-1600s, most of the western coastline of New Holland could be drawn. New Holland was the name the Dutch gave to Australia.

Terra Australis Ignota is Latin for "Unknown Southern Land." An Ancient Greek scholar named Ptolemy (AD 90–168) raised the idea of a southern land. *Australis* means "southern"— as does the name Australia.

COOK'S SECRET ORDERS

James Cook was the captain of a British scientific voyage to Tahiti, but he also had secret orders to search the Pacific Ocean for an unknown southern continent (if one existed in that region). So when Cook completed his work in Tahiti, he sailed directly south into the uncharted waters of the Pacific. But he did not find any land; day after day after day, he found only an empty ocean. So he then turned his ship, the *Endeavour,* to the west. That was the direction of the unexplored land called New Holland.

At 6 a.m. on April 20, 1770, the east coast of New Holland was first seen by Europeans. A week later the *Endeavour* pulled into a harbor that Cook named Botany Bay. He chose this name because of all the new species of plants that were found by the ship's botanist, Joseph Banks.

Over the next four months, Cook mapped the entire east coast of New Holland, claiming the right side of the continent for Britain and naming it New South Wales. When the *Endeavour* finally made it back to England, members of its crew wrote about their discoveries—especially Joseph Banks. He told all of his important friends that New South Wales was a land teeming with exotic plants and animals.

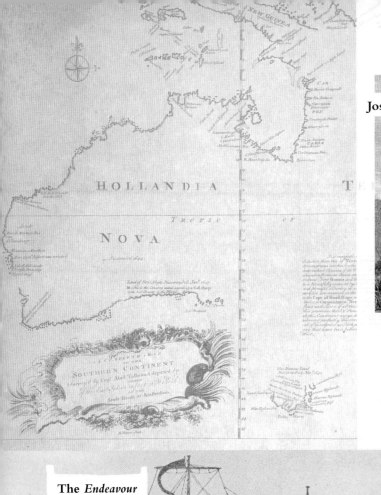

Joseph Banks's kangaroo

Joseph Banks's journal describes his first-ever glimpse of a beast that was as big as a greyhound, had mouse-colored fur and a long tail, and could leap more than six feet (two meters) with each hop of its huge hind legs. The local Aboriginal people called the creature a *gangurru*.

The *Endeavour*

As his landing party pulled onto the sandy shore of Botany Bay, Cook turned to a seventeen-year-old crew member and said, "Jump out, Isaac." Isaac Smith was the first European to set foot on the east coast of Australia. He was a cousin of Cook's wife, Elizabeth. Years later, when James Cook died, Isaac stayed with Mrs. Cook to keep her company.

Captain James Cook

CRIME

At the time when the *Endeavour* returned home, life was miserable for many people in British cities—especially for children from poor families. Disease, filth, and poverty killed thousands of people, and many children were left without parents. If a child could find a job, the work was exhausting, dangerous, and very badly paid.

Why was life so tough? The invention of new machines in the 1700s had changed the way people lived. Mechanical seed planters and plows had improved methods of farming, but they also put a lot of laborers out of work. Thousands of families from rural villages were forced to leave their homes to look for work in overcrowded cities, where new factories were being built. But if jobs weren't available, the poor had only two options: steal or starve. Either way, they could end up dead, because the government had introduced the death penalty for more than two hundred different crimes (even for stealing small items).

Jails were becoming so full that the government decided to use old sailing ships, with their masts removed, as floating prisons called hulks. But when the hulks also became overcrowded, the government needed another solution. Thoughts turned to the possibility of a penal colony, a settlement to which convicted prisoners could be sent as a punishment. For many years a number of European countries—including France, Spain, Portugal, Russia, and the Netherlands—had shipped prisoners to parts of the world that needed cheap labor. Britain, too, had set up penal colonies in places like North America, although these were mostly closed after the American War of Independence (1775–1782).

Around this time, Joseph Banks (among others) suggested that Botany Bay would make a good place for a new penal colony. Banks said this distant land had nice weather and good soil for growing crops, and it was so very far from England that the convicts would never make it back.

A prison hulk

In eighteenth-century Britain, children as young as four went to work. Their tiny bodies made them perfect for cleaning chimneys, working in mines, fixing machinery, and also for breaking into houses. By the age of seven, children were treated the same as adults in British courts. Some were as young as nine years old when they were sentenced to serve punishments such as death by hanging or transportation to Australia.

18th-century England

THE LIFE AND CRIMES OF EDWARD GARDENER

Edward Gardener was a young lad who did not have parents to care for him. He survived, like thousands of other abandoned or orphaned children in the city slums, by joining a gang of thieves. "I belonged to a gang of about twenty-five," he said. "They met at High Street, at a bad house kept by a man named William Hall, who arranged everything and then sent us out. Some were sent to pick pockets, others to rob houses. He used to take us out at night to prey."

MY NAME IS 5418

William Derricourt was a teenager when he was caught stealing a hankie from a judge. In his book, *Old Convict Days,* he described what it was like to be sent to a hulk.

"Before going on board [the hulk] we were stripped to the skin and scrubbed with a hard scrubbing brush. . . . This scrubbing we endured until we looked like boiled lobsters, and the blood was drawn in many places. . . . Our next experience was being marched off to the blacksmith, who riveted on our ankles rings of iron . . . In this rig-out we were transferred to the hulk, where we received our numbers, for no names were used. My number was 5418."

"Sometimes [the children] would neither eat or sleep but wept continuously for three or four days."

—*A prison chaplain*

5

THE FIRST FLEET

Eleven small ships came together in an English harbor before sunrise on Sunday, May 13, 1787. The First Fleet, as we now call it, was setting sail with a human cargo of 759 convicts (including 192 women), along with marines, seamen, and supplies of food and equipment to build a new world. All in all, close to 1,500 people were sailing into the unknown.

Many of the marines kept journals that told of life for the convicts during the eight-month voyage to Botany Bay. They wrote of men like Ishmael Colman, who died when he left England because he was so sad to be sent away. Other records show that twenty-three women had babies while they were at sea and that there was even an attempted mutiny by a couple of convicts (who were given a flogging of twenty-four lashes each when their plot was discovered). But mostly the journey was cramped, boring, smelly, frightening, and, for forty-eight members of the Fleet, also deadly.

When the Fleet finally arrived at Botany Bay, the commander, Captain Arthur Phillip, was disappointed. The soil was not nearly as good as Cook and Banks had reported, and there was a lack of fresh water. Phillip decided to explore farther up the New South Wales coast, and that's where he found what he considered the finest harbor in the world—now known as Sydney Harbor.

On January 26, 1788, Phillip was rowed to shore. A group of convicts looked on from the deck of a nearby ship as Phillip raised the English flag on a post made from a eucalyptus tree. He then named the settlement after the British politician Lord Sydney.

The First Fleet carried livestock, tools, plants, and seeds. But it also carried puppies, kittens, and a piano!

THE LIFE AND CRIMES OF JOHN HUDSON

In England in 1783, a house was broken into, and a shirt, some stockings, a pistol, and some aprons were stolen. But the thief left a clue: on a windowpane were prints of the thief's small, sooty toes. Soon after, a child named John Hudson was caught trying to sell the shirt that had been taken during that burglary. He claimed that his mother had sent him to sell the shirt, which he said belonged to his father, but his court record later showed that this couldn't be true:

COURT TO PRISONER: How old are you?
PRISONER: Going on nine.
COURT: What business were you bred up in?
PRISONER: None. Sometimes chimney sweeping.
COURT: Have you any father and mother?
PRISONER: Dead.
COURT: How long ago?
PRISONER: I don't know.

John was sentenced to seven years' transportation. He was thirteen years old by the time the First Fleet set sail, but he was still the youngest convict on that voyage.

Captain Arthur Phillip raises the British flag at Sydney Cove.

The man in charge of the First Fleet was a navy officer (and part-time farmer) named Arthur Phillip. He wasn't famous or rich, but he was an excellent choice as the first governor of New South Wales because he was fair, disciplined, and well organized.

SEVEN YEARS MEANS LIFE

As well as John Hudson, there were seven other convicts under the age of sixteen on the First Fleet. Elizabeth Hayward, a fourteen-year-old apprentice clog maker, had been sentenced to seven years' transportation for stealing a linen gown and a silk bonnet. She was the youngest convict girl on the voyage.

Like most of the prisoners on the First Fleet, the child convicts were mainly thieves who were sentenced to seven years' transportation—although seven years was actually a life sentence. No one was ever expected to return.

Elizabeth Youngson, fifteen, had originally been sentenced to death for the crime of burglary. It was the same for

Robert Abel, fifteen, who was found guilty of assault and highway robbery. Both had their death sentences reduced to transportation.

Phebe Flarty, fifteen, Ann Mather, fourteen, and Ann Parsley, fifteen, were all transported for stealing clothes, and Charles McLaughlin, fifteen, was found guilty of stealing a purse.

The First Fleet route to Australia

Portsmouth

Rio de Janeiro

Cape of Good Hope

Botany Bay

STARVATION

When convicts like John Hudson and Elizabeth Hayward were rowed to shore at Sydney Cove—and stood on dry land for the first time in about a year—they were met by dense forest known as "bush" . . . and confusion. Everywhere they looked, they would have seen men pitching tents, clearing patches of land, or trying to find covered storage for food supplies. What they *didn't* find was a prison cell, because there were no buildings of any kind in the colony. In fact, it would be many years before John and Elizabeth (like most of the convicts) slept in a real bed again, sat in a chair, or even took shelter under a solid roof—and some convicts would have only the hollow of a tree for their home.

Governor Arthur Phillip hoped the settlement would gradually be able to grow its own food, but nothing went according to plan. The hardwoods of the Australian bush broke many of the convicts' tools; this meant they struggled to clear the land and to cut wood for new buildings. On top of this, there were too few convicts with building or farming skills, and many were too weak to work after the long voyage from England. This was a big problem, because the colony relied on convict labor for its survival—especially when the marines refused to work the land and said their sole job was to protect the colony from invasion.

Then all the crops died; the soil was poor and rocky, the weather baking hot, and the young plants under constant attack from insects and mice. Month after month after month, the convicts, as well as the marines, were forced to survive on the last scraps of rotting food they'd brought with them from England. They even ran out of clothing and shoes, as well as items like candles. Two years after their arrival, many died of hunger.

Could this struggling colony survive? To find out, Phillip gave a freed or "emancipist" farmer named James Ruse two acres of land near Parramatta (west of Sydney). Ruse worked hard on his farm and grew enough food to support his children and his wife, Elizabeth Perry, who had also been transported as a convict on the First Fleet. Ruse was one of the first to prove that agriculture did have a future in this strange land. Following his example, other farms were set up to the west of Sydney. Ruse was also the first to show that hardworking convicts could find a new beginning in New South Wales.

In June 1790, a second fleet of more than 900 convicts arrived in New South Wales, and then a third the following year. The British government sent a message to Phillip to say it would start sending convicts to the colony twice a year. At least this meant that the settlement was guaranteed a regular supply of fresh goods, finally lifting the threat of starvation.

Convict plowing team

When the Fleet first landed, the weekly rations for each man were roughly 7 pounds of salted beef or 4 pounds of pork, 3 pints of dried peas, 7 pounds of bread/flour, 6 ounces of butter, and ½ pound of rice. By April 1790, the weekly rations had been cut back to around 4 pounds of flour, 2½ pounds of pork, and 1½ pounds of rice.

"Famine is staring us in the face . . . and happy is the man that can kill a rat or a crow to make him a dainty meal."

— *New South Wales marine, 1790*

THE LIFE AND CRIMES OF THOMAS BARRETT

It was shortly after his twelfth birthday that Thomas Barrett was caught with a stolen watch and sentenced to death. Eventually, Thomas was shown mercy and was put on a transport ship to Canada, but he escaped before the ship left British waters.

When Thomas was recaptured, he was again sentenced to death and again given mercy. That's how, several years later, he ended up on the First Fleet.

But a few weeks after the convicts arrived in Sydney, Thomas stole butter, a type of porridge known as "pease," and pork from a food tent. For a third time he was sentenced to death, and this time, there was no mercy.

On a warm February afternoon, all the convicts were called together. They watched as Thomas, pale with shock, climbed a ladder and was hanged from a tree.

Thomas Barrett was the first person hanged on Australian soil. With starvation gripping the colony, he wasn't the last.

A LAND WITHOUT PEOPLE?

O ne day on a beach near Sydney Cove, Governor Arthur Phillip found an Aboriginal boy pouring water on the forehead of an old man. Nearby a little girl lay dead near her mother. All four had smallpox blisters and were so thin that they looked as if they were starving. This scene gives us a glimpse of the devastating impact of British settlement on the Aboriginal people.

Before the arrival of the First Fleet, the Australian continent had been populated by only Aboriginal people for more than 50,000 years. In the area around Sydney Cove, there were almost thirty different language and family groups that belonged to and cared for an area of land. Phillip estimated that there might have been around 1,500 Aboriginal people living at the time along that part of the coast. These people suffered greatly when fleets of British ships came to their land; the settlers brought strange diseases with them and caught all the fish from the local waters.

As time passed and it became obvious that the settlers were not going to leave, some of the Aboriginal men began to stand up to the British invaders. One warrior called Pemulwuy led many raids on the British settlement. During one attack, he was shot and wounded. Everyone thought he was going to die. But when Pemulwuy was spotted soon after, he looked as if his wounds had magically disappeared. A legend grew that Pemulwuy could not be killed by the bullets of British guns.

Meanwhile, Phillip desperately wanted to convince some of the Aboriginal people to join his settlement, so he ordered that several local men be kidnapped. A man named Bennelong was one of them. Bennelong quickly learned to speak English and to dress in European clothes. He even moved into a hut at Sydney Cove—on a spot now called Bennelong Point, which is the site of the Sydney Opera House.

Bennelong

The uniforms that were worn by the marines were so strange to the Aboriginal people that they couldn't even tell if the strangers were men or women. To clear up the confusion, one of the marines was ordered to pull down his pants.

In Latin, *Terra nullius* means "a land without people." When the British arrived in Australia, they assumed that the land was empty because the Aboriginal people didn't build farms, houses, or towns. The settlers did not understand the way the Aboriginal people lived.

The Eora people (whose land is what is now the Sydney area) removed a top tooth from their young men at initiation. By coincidence, Governor Arthur Phillip was missing the same front tooth. When the Eora first met Captain Phillip, they thought he may have been the spirit of a dead relative.

A depiction of a *corroboree* of the Eora people

"All they seem'd to want was for us to be gone."

— *Captain James Cook, on first meeting with the Aboriginal people*

PHILLIP'S FAREWELL

Five years after landing in New South Wales, an exhausted Governor Phillip decided to go home. By this time the colony was starting to feed itself. There were more than 3,000 emancipists and free settlers living around Parramatta and Sydney, and 1,700 acres of land were being farmed.

Bennelong was invited by Phillip to join him back in England, where at first Bennelong became a celebrity. He wore lacy shirts, which were the fashion, and he even met the king! But after a couple of English winters, Bennelong became very homesick. Even when he returned to Sydney, he remained sad. Bennelong was lost between two worlds. He never again felt at home with either the British settlers or his own people.

ABOUT CONVICT ORIGINS

New South Wales was the mother colony of Australia, but, as years passed, other settlements were started across the continent.

NEW SOUTH WALES

When Governor Phillip returned to Britain, the military officers of the New South Wales Corps became very powerful. They controlled trade within the colony through payments in rum. The next few governors struggled to control this Rum Corps, as they became known— but while these officers were very greedy, they did help to develop private business and farming within the settlement.

TASMANIA

In 1803, a small group of settlers, including twenty-four convicts, was sent to Van Diemen's Land to stop other nations from claiming the island. These people were the first of 75,000 convicts who would land in Van Diemen's Land over the next fifty years. By the time transportation ended in 1853, Van Diemen's Land had developed a reputation as the home of the very worst convicts. Two years later, the colonists changed the name of the island to Tasmania, hoping for a new beginning.

QUEENSLAND

A penal settlement was set up at Moreton Bay in 1824 so that the New South Wales government could get rid of some of their worst criminals. Patrick Logan became one of the most hated leaders of this settlement because many of his convicts died from being overworked. But one day, Logan was found dead in a shallow grave. The local Aboriginal people were blamed for his murder, but some people believed it was an act of convict revenge. Around 2,280 convicts were sent to this penal settlement before it was eventually replaced by farming communities.

VICTORIA

The British attempted to set up a penal colony at Port Phillip in 1803, but the Sullivan Bay settlement (near present-day Sorrento) was abandoned because of poor soil and a lack of fresh water. Then, in 1835, a Tasmanian farmer named John Batman led a party of free settlers across Bass Strait to look for land. Batman claimed that his group made a deal for the land with the local Aboriginal people in exchange for blankets, knives, scissors, axes, mirrors, and hankies. "Batmania" was the name he gave to the current site of central Melbourne.

WESTERN AUSTRALIA

Many of the first British settlers who sailed to the Swan River were hoping to make it rich on the vast tracts of available land, ignoring the rights of the traditional Aboriginal owners as well as those of the fading Dutch Empire. The isolated colony struggled for years until, in 1849, the settlers asked Britain to send them male convicts as a free source of labor. It was in Western Australia, on January 9, 1868, that the last convict ship (called the *Hougoumont*) unloaded the final 269 convicts.

SOUTH AUSTRALIA

South Australia was set up as a colony for free settlers who were seeking a better life, which was strange, since the idea for the province began with a prisoner in an English jail. Edward Gibbon Wakefield was a writer who had gotten into trouble with the law for running away with a fifteen-year-old girl. Wakefield used his resulting prison time to write newspaper stories about day-to-day life in Sydney—though he'd never been there! These articles made life in the Australian colonies seem so wonderful that plans were made in England for a new and free settlement in South Australia.

THE NORTHERN TERRITORY

The British made several attempts to colonize the coast of what is now called the Northern Territory, but these failed because of the harsh tropical weather and the resistance of the local Aboriginal people. It wasn't until 1869, the year after the final convict boat had docked in Western Australia, that a successful settlement was established at Palmerston, on Port Darwin.

FROM A JAIL TO A COLONY

Life for the convicts began to improve in 1810, when a sandy-haired Scottish man named Lachlan Macquarie became the fifth governor of New South Wales. The next twelve years of his leadership were a turning point for Australia.

Macquarie believed that once convicts had served out their sentences, they deserved the same opportunities as every free man and woman. A convict architect named Francis Greenway became a good example of this: he was employed by Macquarie to design forty stylish buildings, such as the Hyde Park Barracks in Sydney.

It was during the Macquarie era that the first coins were introduced to the colonies and the first bank was opened. Macquarie promoted exploration, agriculture, and expansion to regional areas of New South Wales and Van Diemen's Land, and also set up schools and churches in outlying settlements. Around this time, an export market for Australian wool began to grow and, among the colonies, there was a push for locally elected governments.

Under the leadership of Macquarie, Australians started to believe in the potential of their land—and themselves.

Governor Lachlan Macquarie

"I found New South Wales a jail and left it a colony."
— *Governor Macquarie, 1823*

Hyde Park Barracks

CALLING AUSTRALIA HOME

The name Australia was suggested by Matthew Flinders, a British sailor who was the first man to circumnavigate the southern continent. Governor Macquarie read the book that Flinders wrote about his voyage and also started using the name Australia. By the 1820s, everyone was using it.

Drawing of Close's Sydney, 1817

THE LIFE AND CRIMES OF JAMES BORROW/ MARY REIBEY

James Borrow was thirteen when he was convicted of horse stealing and sentenced to transportation. But when a doctor did a pre-journey medical exam, a shocking discovery was made. James Borrow was actually a girl named Mary Haydock. She'd been living as a boy.

In 1794, a couple of years after arriving in New South Wales, Mary married a trader named Thomas Reibey. He died in 1811, but Mary continued to manage their business while raising their seven children. She did such a good job that she expanded their shipping fleet, built a new warehouse, and soon became one of the wealthiest women in the colony.

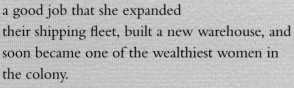

Mary Reibey

Today, Mary Reibey's picture is on the Australian twenty-dollar bill. The country has come to pride itself on being a land of opportunity—one in which even a convict boy could become a leading businesswoman.

Cameras did not exist in the early 1800s, but an artist named Edward Close drew this picture of Sydney in 1817. His illustration shows (left to right) a government official, an emancipist, a well-to-do free settler, a musician from a military band, a soldier, a government convict, another free settler, another government convict, another soldier, and a convict overseer.

WHAT WORKS BEST?

Overseers found that the secret to getting the best work out of the convicts was to reward good behavior. The hardest-working convicts were often allowed to grow and sell their own crops, hire themselves out as tradesmen in their spare time, and even apply for their families to be sent over from Britain.

There were fewer opportunities for boys because they lacked the strength needed for hard labor. In the early 1820s, a barracks for convict boys, called the Carters' Barracks, was built on the Sydney Brickfields (now Central Station). Some of these boys became helpers for the convict gangs of brickmakers, while others were given the chance to be apprenticed to the site's carpenter, shoemaker, stonecutter, or blacksmith.

PUNISHMENT

A convict boy named Edward Scandrick was about fourteen years old when his ship, the *Mangles,* arrived in New South Wales. He was sent to live at Carters' Barracks, on the Sydney Brickfields. But one morning Edward said he felt too sick to go to work, and his guards did not believe him. Edward was charged with neglect of duty and sentenced to twenty-five lashes with a cat-o'-nine-tails (a type of whip). A government witness said that Edward had also received fifty lashes the week before. "Blood came from the first stroke," wrote the witness. "[Edward] screamed dreadfully at every lash; the blood running freely from the old wounds; he lost much blood."

We don't know a lot about boys like Edward, but we do know that flogging was a common form of punishment within the convict system. Surprisingly, it was the punishment for minor offenses such as being rude or drunk, or not turning up to work. Convicts could be flogged with twenty-five, fifty, seventy-five, or one hundred lashes, although some men were given up to one thousand lashes—so many that the bones were exposed in their shredded backs.

HELL ON EARTH

Another form of punishment was to be sent to a penal station, which was a settlement where convicts were forced to do hard labor and were constantly watched. The most feared of all the penal settlements were those at Port Arthur and Norfolk Island.

Punishment at the brutal prison outpost on Norfolk Island, in the Pacific Ocean, was the toughest you could get, short of death. The convicts were subjected to a lack of food (sometimes only one meal every two days), constant hard labor, filthy living conditions, and even torture.

The largest of the penal stations was at Port Arthur, in Van Diemen's Land (Tasmania). The convicts at Port Arthur were flogged so often that it became a badge of honor. A separate prison was built for their mental torture; the convicts were locked alone in cells for months and not allowed to talk to (or even look at) another human being.

Convict flogging

Some convicts were placed in leg irons for one to two years, and it was a punishment that usually went along with hard labor. Leg irons were also used to chain convicts together in gangs, preventing them from escaping while they worked to build roads. The heaviest leg irons weighed up to forty pounds (eighteen kilograms).

Most convicts wore the same clothes that they were wearing when they were sentenced, but the worst-behaved convicts at the penal settlements wore a multicolored "magpie" outfit in the style of a jester or a clown. It was intended to make the convict feel ridiculous and ashamed. Convict clothes could also be marked with the King's Broad Arrow, which showed they belonged to the British government.

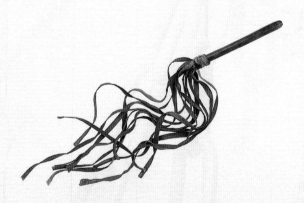

The cat-o'-nine-tails was a whip with nine pieces of rope that ripped the flesh from the backs of its victims. The person being punished was tied to a triangular frame and whipped.

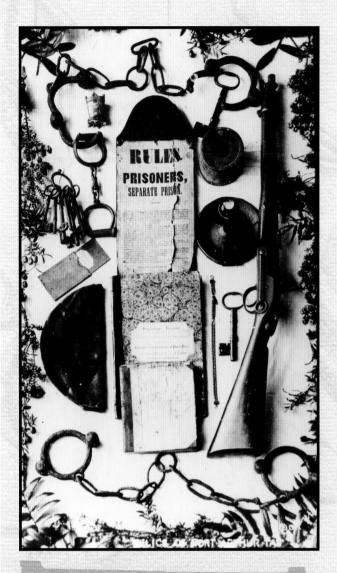

THE LIFE AND CRIMES OF WILLIAM WESTWOOD

William Westwood was fifteen years old when he was transported for stealing a coat. He spent every minute of the next ten years trying to escape—at first from the farm where he was sent to work, and then from Port Arthur. When he was eventually sent to Norfolk Island, he led the convicts in a murderous revolt.

"I welcome death as a friend," William wrote when he was sentenced to be hanged for murder. "I have been treated more like a beast than a man."

In the days before he died, William cut a single curl from his head and sent it back to his family. All he ever wanted, he wrote in his final letter, was to "regain my freedom and visit my dear . . . parents and friends again."

BOYS WILL BE BOYS

Ten years after the Carters' Barracks was built in Sydney, a separate prison for boys was set up in Van Diemen's Land near the dreaded Port Arthur settlement—but instead of simply housing the boys, this project attempted to rehabilitate them. The Point Puer prison was the first one anywhere in the British Empire in which child inmates were given training in a trade, lessons in math and reading, and religious guidance about how to be a good person.

DRUNK!

When the first sixty-eight Point Puer boys were shipped to the prison from Hobart in January 1834, they broke into the ship's storage and found seventy-two bottles of wine (belonging to the commandant of Port Arthur). The boys drank nearly all the bottles and were "in a perfectly senseless state" when they finally arrived.

IN SHEEP'S CLOTHING

Point Puer boys wore jackets and pants made of sheepskin, along with a striped shirt and a leather cap. They were not given any underwear or socks (but they sometimes put hand towels in their boots).

Point Puer

- - - - - - **90-168** - - - - - - - - - -
Ancient Greek scholar
Ptolemy raises the idea
of *Terra Australis.*

- - - - **1606** - - - -
Willem Janszoon, Dutch
sea captain, lands on the
southern continent.

- **APRIL 1770** - - - - -
Europeans first sight the
east coast of New Holland.

THE DAILY ROUTINE

5:30 a.m.: Boys are woken. They roll up their bedding, pray, and then wash in the freezing-cold sea. They march to work in the settlement garden.

8:15 a.m.: A breakfast of bread and gruel (watery porridge) is served.

9:30 a.m.: Boys are sent to work at trades.

1 p.m.: A lunch of more bread and gruel is served.

2 p.m.: Boys return to trade work.

5 p.m.: Boys go back to their barracks for a dinner of salted beef or pork, served with a pudding of flour and fatty water (the liquid that the meat was boiled in). Turnips and cabbage are sometimes served.

6:30 p.m.: School.

8 p.m.: Prayer, roll call, and bed.

The boys' prison was called Point Puer because *puer* is Latin for "youth."

GAMES

The boys did not have any personal belongings or toys, so they made up their own games. One of their favorites was to make a row of buttons (which they removed from their clothes) and then use another button to knock each one out of the line. The aim of most games was to gamble on the result, with the winner collecting all of the buttons.

As many as 3,000 boys, between the ages of nine and eighteen, passed through Point Puer before it was shut down in 1849.

THE LIFE AND CRIMES OF WALTER PAISLEY

When Walter Paisley was thirteen, he was around four feet (125 centimeters) tall, the height of an average eight-year-old today. His older brother Francis and four friends chose Walter to be lowered through an open window to break into a house. But when Walter was caught, the others ran away. "I was the only one tried," Walter said. "The rest could not be found."

Walter was one of the first boys sent to Point Puer—and the most rebellious. Over the next five years, forty charges were made against his name, and he spent an average of more than two days of every month in solitary confinement (locked alone in a dark cell on a diet of bread and water).

Walter was locked up for being disobedient, telling rude stories, smuggling tobacco to a friend who was in solitary confinement, singing filthy songs, punching his teacher, breaking his work in the carpenter's shop, hitting a fellow boy with a spade, and stealing a chicken from the schoolmaster.

AUGUST 22, 1770
Cook claims the east coast for Britain.

1771
The *Endeavour* arrives back in England.

1786
Captain Arthur Phillip is chosen to set up a penal colony at Botany Bay.

ESCAPE

Thomas Davis was a sixteen-year-old factory worker in England when he was found guilty of stealing a small amount of money. It was the second time he'd been caught, and perhaps that's why he received the tough sentence of transportation for life. But this was just the beginning of Thomas's story.

While in Van Diemen's Land, Thomas twice attempted to escape from Port Arthur. He was sentenced to a total of 275 lashes for these (and other) offenses. He then tried to run away when he was assigned to work for a free settler, and again when he was sent to work in a government road gang. For this effort, he was sentenced to twelve months' hard labor in chains. Thomas's fifth attempt to run ended when he was caught with a forged certificate of freedom.

We don't know what happened next to Thomas, except for a final entry on his convict record: "RUN." Was his sixth attempt to escape finally successful?

What we do know for sure is that the thought of freedom was a constant dream for the convicts transported to Australia.

Convict chain gang

MAY 13, 1787
The First Fleet, led by Phillip, leaves England for Australia.

JANUARY 18, 1788
Phillip reaches Botany Bay but doesn't find it suitable.

JANUARY 21, 1788
Phillip explores Sydney Harbor.

SHIPWRECKED

One of the most famous convict escapes was in the early years of settlement when a young woman named Mary Bryant—along with her husband, William, their two young children, and a group of friends—stole a small boat from Sydney Cove and sailed north. They covered more than 3,000 miles (5,000 kilometers) in sixty-nine days, surviving thirst, starvation, and dangerous seas. When the escapees finally arrived in Timor, they told everyone that they were survivors of a shipwreck. This lie didn't work for long.

The escapees were shipped back to England to stand trial, but Mary's husband and children died during the journey. The British public admired Mary when they heard of her daring escape and also felt sad that she'd lost her children. Because of this public support, she was given her freedom.

HAVING A FRIEND FOR DINNER

Alexander Pearce was in a group of convicts that escaped from a brutal penal settlement at Macquarie Harbor, on the west coast of Van Diemen's Land. After walking for a couple of weeks without food, the members of the gang started killing and eating one another. Pearce was the last man standing.

When Pearce was finally captured, he was sent back to Macquarie Harbor. But a year later he escaped again, this time with a convict named Thomas Cox. Pearce gave himself up after five days. He'd had a piece of pork, some bread, and a few fish at his camp—but Cox had been the main course! "Human flesh was by far preferable," Pearce confessed before he was hanged. He added that the thick part of the arm was quite delicious.

I'LL FORGIVE YOU

Joseph Johns was better known by the nickname Moondyne Joe. He escaped so often from Western Australian work gangs that an "escape-proof" cell was made for him at Fremantle Prison. When Governor John Hampton inspected this cell—which was made from stone, lined with hardwood lumber and held together with more than 1,000 nails—he joked that if Moondyne Joe escaped again, he'd forgive him. Moondyne Joe didn't exactly escape from this cell, but he did slip away through a hole that he dug in the wall of an exercise yard. He was on the run for two years before he was caught—and no, he wasn't forgiven.

Moondyne Joe

JANUARY 26, 1788
Phillip moves the Fleet to Sydney Cove and raises the British flag.

NOVEMBER 1789
James Ruse is the first ex-convict to get a land grant.

1790
Famine strikes the colony and nearly a quarter of the settlers die.

MOTHERS OF THE NATION

In April 1853, a ship named the *Duchess of Northumberland* sailed into Hobart, carrying Australia's last cargo of female convicts. In the years after the arrival of the First Fleet, around 25,000 women had been transported to New South Wales and Van Diemen's Land. Most of these women were poor and had been convicted of stealing.

Of all the women transported over the years, only a few hundred were under the age of sixteen. More than half were between seventeen and twenty-nine.

Nearly all convict women, at some time during their sentence, would have been sent to a "female factory." Female factories were places of punishment for crimes such as being drunk, getting pregnant, or running away from a job. Women in this section of the prison wore a big yellow *C* on their clothes to show that they belonged to the lowest class. Hospital care was also provided at the female factories for sick and pregnant women. But it wasn't a nice place to have a baby, because the unmarried mothers could have their food rations cut to punish them for becoming pregnant. Many babies died from the poor diet and filthy living conditions.

Some women simply lived at the female factory while they were waiting to be assigned to a settler, for whom they would work as a servant in the kitchen, laundry, or garden. Their duties may have included washing clothes by hand in local rivers or preparing a vegetable patch.

Many female factories could be found in the colonies, but the first was set up in Parramatta, west of Sydney. Women at the Parramatta Female Factory worked for the region's wool industry by spinning wool and weaving it into cloth. At the Cascades Female Factory, which was the biggest of its kind, the women provided laundry services for the Hobart settlement.

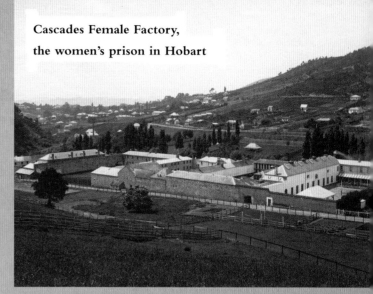

Cascades Female Factory, the women's prison in Hobart

JUNE 1790
The arrival of the Second Fleet.

JULY 1791
The Third Fleet arrives.

1803
Settlement established in Van Diemen's Land.

In April 1838, an inquest was held into the death of a convict at the Cascades Female Factory in Hobart. The jury in this inquest asked to inspect the female factory because they'd heard rumors of dead children being smuggled out of the buildings. The record of what they saw is frightening: the babies in the nursery were sickly and miserable; the dark, damp cells were described as "most frightful dungeons"; and the solitary cells were so smelly that it forced some jurors to run from the building, gasping for air.

A female house of correction was a place of punishment, and the punishment was mostly in the form of hard work. That's why these institutions were known as "female factories."

Flogging women was outlawed in 1817, but there were other forms of punishment. Some women were humiliated by having their heads shaved, while others had uncomfortable iron collars locked around their necks.

THE LIFE AND CRIMES OF MARY WADE

Mary Wade was ten when she was sentenced to death by hanging. Mary and a friend had attacked an eight-year-old girl, broken her drink bottle, and stolen her clothes. Mary's sentence was eventually reduced to transportation, and she arrived in New South Wales in 1790.

By the time Mary was fourteen, she'd had a baby with an Irish convict. Two more children followed, but then this man left the colony. Mary then set up house with a man named Jonathan Brooker. The couple married when they were granted their freedom, and Mary had many more babies—twenty-one in total.

When Mary died at age 82, she had more than 300 descendants. Today her descendants number in the tens of thousands—and a former Australian prime minister, Kevin Rudd, is one of them.

SHOPPING FOR A WIFE

All through the convict years, there were many more men in the colonies than women—only one out of every five convicts who arrived in Australia before 1823 was a woman. One of the more unusual ways that a man could meet a woman was at a female factory. A man named Patrick Clark went to a female factory one day and told the doctor there that he wanted a wife. "A mate of mine got one here twelve months ago, and she has proved a good one," he said. It took Patrick two minutes to decide that a convict named Alice McCabe was the girl for him. They married and lived happily ever after.

Convict couple

1810
Governor Lachlan Macquarie arrives in New South Wales. At the time, there were nearly 12,000 people of British origin in the colonies of New South Wales and Van Diemen's Land.

1803
Matthew Flinders becomes the first explorer to sail around Australia.

1813
The first batch of merino wool is exported from Sydney to England.

THE END OF TRANSPORTATION

In the 1830s, the eastern colonies of Australia became wealthy from agriculture. Free settlers sailed from Britain for the chance of a better life, and native-born Australians (mostly the children of convicts) grew into honest and hardworking people. These currency lads and lasses, as they were called (named after the first coins in the colonies), grew taller, stronger, and healthier than their relatives back in Britain—mostly because the food was better in Australia, the warmer weather meant that everyone could enjoy an outdoor lifestyle, and there was lots of work available for people on which to thrive.

But while the free settlers and native-born Australians disliked the convict image, the main impetus to end transportation came from within Britain. This was because:

* some people said transportation was too similar to slavery;

* the threat of transportation no longer stopped others from committing crimes because hundreds of free people were choosing to settle in Australia; and

* many people in Britain started to argue that nothing good could come from dumping all of these convicts in one place (but they were wrong).

In May 1840, the British government removed New South Wales from the list of places they sent convicts. The final convict ship arrived in Van Diemen's Land in May 1853.

Nearly 10,000 men were transported to Western Australia between 1850 and 1868. The last convict did not serve out his sentence in Fremantle Prison until 1906.

THE FINAL NUMBERS

Between 1788 and 1868, Britain sent around 162,000 convicts to Australia on 806 ships. Meanwhile, 58,000 free migrants sailed to Australia between 1815 and 1840. By 1851, there were about 400,000 people in the Australian colonies, most of them free.

End of transportation commemorative coin

1820
There are 24,000 people of British origin in New South Wales.

1824
Prison settlement established at Moreton Bay.

1829
British government establishes the Swan River Colony. The entire continent is now claimed to be part of the British Empire.

During the gold rush, the immigrants who came to Australia were middle class.

GOLD FEVER!

In 1851, gold was found in New South Wales and Victoria. In the following year alone, gold fever brought more than 370,000 people to Australia—that's more than double the number of convicts that had been transported over the previous seventy years.

The discovery of gold was one of the final reasons that transportation ended. The British government could no longer punish criminals with a trip to Australia when thousands of free people were rushing there to find their fortune.

The iron of convict chains had shaped the beginnings of modern Australia, but the story was about to be transformed by a more precious metal.

John West was a church minister who opposed transportation. His views were supported by people from all the different Australian colonies, and in 1851, the Australasian Anti-Transportation League was formed. This was the first time that people from all the different Australian colonies came together for a single purpose. John West designed this flag for the group. It was a hint of what would happen fifty years later, when the six colonies voted to form the nation of Australia.

AUSTRALASIAN LEAGUE.

TASMANIA.

INSTITUTED 1851.

1830
A penal settlement at
Port Arthur is established.

1834
British Parliament passes
an act to establish the
province of South Australia.

1835
John Batman explores
Port Phillip Bay.

25

TODAY'S CONVICT LINKS

In the 1870s, just before Port Arthur closed as a prison, a photographer was invited behind the walls to record the faces of its last convicts. Transportation to the eastern colonies had ended twenty years before. These old men, who were too sick or disturbed to leave the prison, were not typical of the young convicts who had helped build a nation. But still, their faces are haunting. In their distant expressions we see the brutal origins of modern Australia.

Some countries were colonized because they were rich in precious metals. Others offered religious freedom. Modern Australia was a dumping ground for British criminals—it may not sound good, but it is a story of survival. For the convicts who overcame the heartbreak of being torn from their homes and sent across the world, a reward was on offer: the prize was opportunity. More than two hundred years later, this same promise continues to draw people from all the nations of the world to the Great Southern Land.

Photographs of Port Arthur prisoners

1840
The end of transportation to New South Wales.

1850
Convict transportation to Western Australia begins.

1851
Gold rushes begin in New South Wales and Victoria.

THE MOTHER COUNTRY

From 1850 onward, the Australian colonies gained their own parliaments, and in 1901, the Commonwealth of Australia was created. But even today, the queen or king of Britain remains its official head of state. This connection dates back to the origins of the First Fleet.

MABO

The concept of *terra nullius,* which was the excuse used by British settlers to take Aboriginal land, was overthrown by the High Court of Australia in 1992. This case was based on a land claim by an Aboriginal man named Eddie Koiki Mabo, and it recognized the rights of Australia's indigenous peoples to their lands.

AUSTRALIAN CONVICT SITES

In 2010, eleven Australian convict sites were recognized as a UNESCO World Heritage site:
* Kingston and Arthur's Vale Historic Island (Norfolk Island)
* Old Government House and Domain (NSW)
* Hyde Park Barracks (NSW)
* Brickendon–Woolmers Estates (Tasmania)
* Darlington Probation Station (Tasmania)
* Old Great North Road (NSW)
* Cascades Female Factory (Tasmania)
* Port Arthur Historic Site (Tasmania)
* Coal Mines Historic Site (Tasmania)
* Cockatoo Island Convict Site (NSW)
* Fremantle Prison (WA)

The interior of a church in Port Arthur

1853
Final convicts arrive in Van Diemen's Land.

1856
Van Diemen's Land is renamed Tasmania.

1868
Australia's final cargo of transported convicts arrives in Western Australia.

GLOSSARY

architect: person who designs structures, like buildings

assigned convict: convict sent to work for a settler

botanist: person who studies plants

certificate of freedom: certificate given to a convict when his or her sentence had ended

commandant: commanding officer

continents: the main landmasses on earth

convict/convicted prisoner: prisoner sentenced to hard labor

corroboree: Aboriginal ceremonies that involve singing and dancing

death penalty: the punishment of being put to death for committing a crime

descendant: a relative of someone from the past

emancipist: a convict who is free after serving his or her sentence or having received a pardon

Eora: one of the Aboriginal groups who are the traditional owners of land near Sydney Harbor

exotic: plants and animals that are foreign

governor: a person appointed by the British government to lead a colony

initiation: a ceremony in which a person is accepted into a group

marine: naval troops who served on ships and on land

mutiny: a plan to overthrow the leader of a group (like the captain of a ship)

New South Wales Corps: a military group sent out with the Second Fleet to preserve law and order in New South Wales

pease: a porridge of squashed peas

penal: in reference to a place of confinement and punishment of prisoners

rehabilitate: to change someone for the better

road gang/chain gang: a group of convicts ordered to work in leg irons

smallpox: a disease caused by a virus with symptoms that include a severe rash and fever

southern hemisphere: the southern half of the earth

transportation: sending prisoners to a British colony as punishment for a crime

voyage: a long journey to distant places

REFERENCES

BIBLIOGRAPHY

Bogle, Michael. *Convicts: Transportation & Australia.* Sydney: Historic Houses Trust of New South Wales, 2008.

Clark, Manning. *A Short History of Australia.* Sydney: Macmillan, 1982.

Female Factory Research Group. *Convict Lives: Women at Cascades Female Factory.* Tasmania: Research Tasmania, 2009.

Hill, David. *1788: The Brutal Truth of the First Fleet.* North Sydney, N.S.W.: William Heinemann, 2008.

Hirst, J. B. *Convict Society and Its Enemies.* Sydney: Allen & Unwin, 1983.

Keneally, Thomas. *Australians: Origins to Eureka (Vol. 1).* Sydney: Allen & Unwin, 2009.

Maxwell-Stewart, Hamish, and Susan Hood. *Pack of Thieves? 52 Port Arthur Lives.* Port Arthur, Tasmania: Port Arthur Historic Site Management Authority, 2010.

Pridmore, Walter B. *Point Puer . . . and the Prisons of Port Arthur.* Murdunna, Tasmania: WB Pridmore, 2005.

IMAGE CREDITS

INDEX